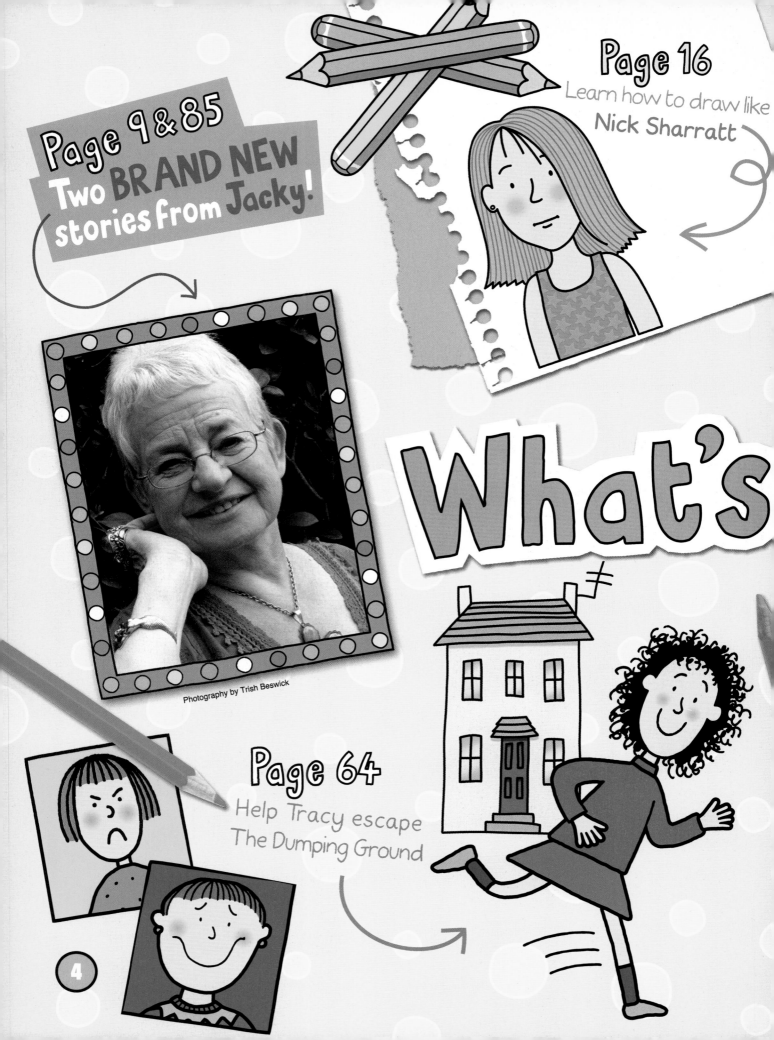

What's

Photography by Trish Beswick

Inside...

All About Me!

This annual belongs to:

I am .... **years old**

Your Secrets!

My favourite colour is:

My favourite book is:

The most embarrassing thing that happened to me was:

When I grow up I want to be: --

I like eating: --

I am happiest when: --

My biggest fear is: --

My best friend is:

....

Her favourite animal is:

....

She loves the colour: ....

I'm the only one that knows she: ....

....

Her favourite book is: ....

Your Best Friend!

Draw a picture of you and your bestie here

Jacky's Christmas This or That

Find out what Jacky loves about Christmas!

Real tree or fake tree?

Real tree EVERY time (in spite of the mess on the carpet).

Parsnips or Brussels sprouts?

I love both! And lots of roast potatoes.

Santa or Frosty the Snowman?

Santa — because he brings lots of presents!

Do you like to get presents or vouchers?

I prefer presents, they are somehow so much more special.

Star or fairy on the top of the tree?

I have a Christmas fairy at the top of my tree.

Christmas pudding or trifle?

Neither. I prefer fresh fruit salad and cream.

Pantomime or carol concert?

Carol concert, especially if there's a children's choir.

Do you peek at your pressies — yes or no?

No, I'm a very good girl. I don't peek — though I might sometimes squeeze!

Deck the Halls or Silent Night?

Silent Night — it's so beautiful.

Christmas at home or away?

Christmas is always at home — but I would love to get away somewhere warm one year.

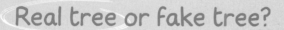

8

Jacqueline Wilson

Knocking The Head Off An Alien

Illustrated by Nick Sharratt

Read and Review!
Colour the stars to rate this story ⟿

I came home from school to find a two metre tall rabbit staring at itself in my mum's wardrobe mirror. It gave a little squeal when it spotted me. I gave a little squeal too, though I'm not usually a squeally sort of person.

'Oh Noel, you gave me a fright creeping up on me like that!' said the rabbit, trying to pull its head off.

I'm Noel. Like 'The first Noel the angel did say...' It's what everyone sings when I tell them my name. The first thing they say is 'I bet you were born on Christmas day, right?' Wrong! I was born in July. (My birthday was actually in five days time and I was looking forward to it like anything.)

Mum called me Noel after her favourite writer when she was a little girl. That's typical of Mum. She's a librarian. I know exactly what name I'd have been saddled with if I'd been a boy. Roald.

'Oh no. It's stuck!' said the rabbit, tugging and twisting its head.

'Come here,' I said, sighing. I reached up and got hold of both ears.

'Careful! Don't pull them off!' said the rabbit.

One quick flick and I had the huge furry head in my arms. My mother's own face, very pink and damp, blinked at me from the top of the giant rabbit get-up.

'Honestly, Mum! You don't half look a twit,' I said.

'I know,' said Mum, trying to wriggle out of the rest of it.

'You're not going to appear in public like that?' I said.

Mum nodded.

'Maria said she'd do the rabbit story-telling session, but now her twins have gone down with chicken-pox so she can't possibly come to the Summer Fun Day.'

So when is this super fun event?' I said, helping Mum skin herself.

Mum looked at me anxiously...

'Mum?'

'Well, it's this Saturday, Noel.'

'But that's my birthday! We're going to the Flowerfields Shopping Centre. And we're having lunch at McDonalds, and then we're going to a film. You promised!'

'I know,' said Mum. 'And we'll still do it all — after the library fun day. Oh Noel, I'm sorry.'

Mum paused, one leg still trapped in rabbit skin. 'Please say you don't mind too much.'

'I mind heaps,' I said. 'Look, you go and tweak your ears and waggle your powder-puff tail. I'll stay at home and watch telly till you're through.'

'You can't stay at home by yourself without anyone to look after you,' said Mum. 'Oh, blow this silly costume.' She gave the leg a last tug, toppled, and fell thump on her bottom.

'You're the one who needs looking after,' I said, unhooking her leg and picking her up. 'Okay, okay, I'll go. Just don't expect me to have fun, okay?'

Mum woke me early on Saturday with a little pile of presents. I felt them all first. 'Don't worry, there isn't a single book,' said Mum.

She's given up on me with books. When I was little we had story sessions all day long and it was like I was permanently caged in a zoo with Little Bear and The Very Hungry Caterpillar and The Tiger Who Came To Tea and Frances the Badger and Elmer the Elephant and all the Wild Things. It was okay, I suppose – but then I got big enough to read to myself and somehow I couldn't be bothered, I'd always much sooner watch telly or play on a computer. Mum tried s-o-o-o-o hard to find me the right book that would spark off the reading habit. Now she pretends she doesn't mind a bit. Ha!

She gave me two DVDs for my birthday. 'Little Women' and 'A Little Princess'. I tried to look enthusiastic. (Maybe I could whip them back to the shop and swap them for some wondrously gory horror movies?).

The last present was much better – a pair of Nike trainers. Mostly I have to make do with Tesco cheapies so this was seriously special.

'You are a mega-great mother,' I said, giving her a hug.

I had cards and smelly stuff from Lush and music tokens and chocolates and a game and some gel pens from my friends. Nothing at all from my father.

'Don't say he's forgotten again,' Mum said wearily. 'I'll phone him up. It's too bad of him.'

'No, it's great, because he'll feel so guilty when you tell him he'll probably send me a whacking great cheque,' I said.

I can act really cool about my parents splitting up. Well, nowadays. We're fine, Mum and me. Just so long as she doesn't muck things up with a boyfriend. There's this Total Drip who works at the library and fusses round her.

He was fussing in overdrive when Mum and I arrived at the park where the Fun Day was being held, setting up all the stalls and dashing around being drippily keen and enthusiastic. I assumed his amazingly nerdy woolly cap was his own personal choice of headgear – but Mum told me he was being Wally.

'Yes, he's being a right wally if you ask me,' I said.

Mum gave me a nudge.

'He's being the Wally. You know, in the *Where's Wally* books? He's going to hide among the crowds and give every child a lollipop if they can spot him,' said Mum.

I felt Mum was being a bit optimistic. The crowds were rather thin on the ground so far. While she struggled into her rabbit costume in the library van I wandered round the stalls, yawning. There were book quizzes galore, a face painting stall, a *Charlie and the Chocolate Factory* sweet stall, a fairy tale bouncy castle, an author's signing table, all the usual stuff. Plus there was a strange sort of coconut shy, only there weren't any coconuts, just painted green heads set up on sticks.

'Knock the head off an Alcazar Alien,' said Jenny, one of my mum's mates at the library.

'Knock the head off a *what*?' I said.

'You know, Noel. Haven't you read the Alcazar Science Fantasy series? You'd love them. They're very popular with kids who... who don't like reading very much.' She lowered her voice as she said the last bit, as if it was a serious social disease.

I laughed.

'No thanks,' I said. 'But I'll have a go at knocking the head off one of the Ally Alien thingies.'

It wasn't as easy as I'd thought. I'm usually absolutely ace at coconut shies but these little green alien heads were jammed so firmly on to their stands one didn't even wobble when I hit it first go. I don't like to admit defeat. So I had another go and another and another. Jenny said I didn't have to pay as my mum was staff. Besides, I was good at drumming up custom.

There were quite a lot of people in the park now. No-one seemed particularly interested in spotting the sad substitute Wally – and sadly not a lot of kids were surrounding the rabbit in the story-time corner. But there were heaps gathering round the alien shy – and it was a good job I'm not shy because most of them were watching me. I was getting the knack of it now. I worked out how to get enough spin on the ball to catch the alien head whack, just where its temple would be – and it shot up and keeled off its stand with a satisfying kerplonk. All the kids cheered.

I queued up again but didn't get so lucky the next time. There were masses and masses of people in the park now, mostly clustered round this stall. The next time I felled two alien heads with just three balls.

'Wow! You've definitely hit the jackpot, Noel. Here's your prize,' said Jenny.

I was pretty chuffed – until I saw what the prize was. A paperback omnibus of Alcazar Alien stories.

'Oh yuck!' I said.

'Yuck?' said this guy standing nearby, with this great cluster of kids all around him.

I wondered if he was their school teacher or something, though he didn't look a bit teachery in his black shirt and black jeans. He looked pretty fit. Maybe he was some celebrity footballer (with a new book of football tips?) Mum's colleagues had somehow duped into attending their Fun Day? But then I'd surely recognise him? He looked so cool, with his tousled blonde hair and dark brown eyes. No, cancel the footballer idea, this guy could well be a rock star (here to publicise his book of greatest hits?). Yes, because lots of the kids had autograph books.

'I take it you don't go a bundle on the Alcazar omnibus?' this guy said to me.

Jenny was blushing and mouthing stuff at me. I felt a bit embarrassed. I didn't want to come across as this really rude ungrateful bratty kid (though three wins ought to have a Mega-Great Triple Whammy Prize – not just a boring old book).

'Well, I haven't ever read this stuff,' I said.

'You'll love the Alcazar stories, you really will,' said Jenny, bright-red in the face.

I didn't see why she was making such a big thing of it.

'You know I'm not really into books,' I said. 'I find reading pretty boring, actually.'

'Noel!' Jenny squeaked, in seeming agony.

'Don't you know who he is?' said one of the kids, sniggering at me. 'He's Peter Foster.'

It didn't connect at first. Peter Foster, footballer, rock star...? Then I saw a name in big silver letters on the Alcazar book. Peter Foster, author!

'Oh gosh,' I said, going hot all over.

But it was okay. He didn't look a bit offended. He was laughing.

'I find writing pretty boring a lot of the time,' he said. 'Don't worry, Noel. I don't mind a bit if you don't read my book. I'm sure you've got heaps of more interesting things to do. You're obviously a girl of action. You've certainly got a really lethal way of bowling. I think we'd all better watch our heads!'

I shuffled my feet in my new Nike trainers, thrilled that he was being so cool.

'Maybe I'll give the book a go after all, seeing as it's by you,' I said. 'Would you sign it for me?'

So he wrote: 'To Noel, who is not my number one fan! I promise you don't have to read this book. Yours, Peter Foster' and he did a little picture of himself too, a tiny stylish pin man all in black, waving at me.

I showed it to Mum. She squinted through her rabbit eyes and said, 'Oh, isn't that lovely of him. But I hope you weren't too cheeky.'

'I didn't mean to be cheeky. I just didn't twig who he was at first.' I was flicking through the first few pages. It didn't look too difficult. There were lots of talky bits – and he didn't seem to take this space stuff too seriously. I read one really funny paragraph and giggled.

I looked up. The rabbit was peering at me.

'Okay, okay,' I said. 'I'll give it a try.'

'Good,' said Mum.

She tried to sound ever so casual. Her rabbit head stayed immobile. But I could tell she was practically clapping her bunny paws together in glee.

I read the entire omnibus over the weekend (and there wasn't much of Saturday left after we'd finished at the Fun Day and had our Big Macs and french fries and pottered round the Flowerfields Shopping Centre and been to a film – a truly scary creepy horror movie. Mum ended up hiding her head in my lap!)

Dad sent a cheque the next week. A big one, just as I'd predicted! I bought myself a new football strip – and several Peter Foster paperbacks. I looked in the library too, but they were in such demand I could never find them on the shelves.

I read them in a great happy rush. Old Jenny was right for once. Then I phoned her up and wheedled Peter Foster's address from her.

I wrote him this letter, telling him I'd read his book after all, lots of his books, and guess what – maybe I was his number one fan after all!

THE END

TOP SECRET
– Nick Tells All!

Pencils or paints?

Of all the different ways I create images the most satisfactory for me is drawing on a sheet of white paper with a plain old pencil.

Seaside or city?

I live on the coast and I can look out to sea from my living room window. It has a very calming effect.

Ruby or Garnet?

I drew her illustrations in Double Act. My illustrator friend Sue Heap did Garnet's illustrations, but she deliberately drew in a similar style to mine, just to confuse everyone. Like the twins do to poor Rose!

Cats or dogs?

They don't bark or dribble all over you.

Walk or drive?

It's much better for you — and the planet!

Computer or paper?

This is a tough choice. I love doing my colouring on a computer — for me a computer is like a magical bumper pack of felt tip pens that never run out! But I have to do the actual drawing the old fashioned way, on paper, and the drawing bit is my favourite part.

Sweets or crisps?

I have a very sweet tooth! Giant chocolate buttons and Liquorice Allsorts are my current favourites.

felt tips

Birthday or Christmas?

Mine's in the middle of summer and it's so nice to spend it outside in the sunshine.

birthday cake

yum!

Rock or pop?

My favourite kind of music is 70's disco — the cheesier the better!

My How To Draw Art File

Learn how to draw Nick Sharratt–style!

What's Inside–

Get ready to amaze with your super drawing skills!

Art File

Best Friends

File

Puzzles & Games

Make & Create

STORY SCHOOL

How To Draw Lily

Draw just like Nick!

1 Draw a half-egg shape for Lily's face and sketch in a long curving line for her hair. Add in her neck and shoulders.

2 Sketch three lines for her fringe and add her ear. Draw a simple vest top shape on Lily's body and complete the outline of her hair.

3 Add in the details on Lily's face in fine black pen and use a zig-zag line to finish the bottom of her hair. Don't forget to add her earring! Finally, use a blue felt tip to draw lots of tiny star outlines on her top.

4 Now you can colour her in! Lily has light brown hair and her top is pink with blue stars.

16

Tip: You can draw your own design on Lily's top to give her a new look.

Draw Lily here!

My How To Draw Art File

17

Mandy Makeover

Get creative and give Mandy a cool new look!

Mandy really doesn't like the babyish outfits her mum dresses her in and wishes she could wear glamorous clothes like her new best friend, Tanya. Draw a fantastic new outfit for Mandy and make her dreams come true! Here are some top tips to give you inspiration:

Dress To Impress

You can be as imaginative as you like with Mandy's new outfit: a girlie party dress; funky flared jeans with a bright vest top; fun dungarees with flowery patches; or how about a uniform? Transform Mandy into a doctor with a stethoscope, a decorator in overalls or a policewoman with handcuffs!

Fancy Feet

Will you give Mandy cool new trainers, strappy sandals, practical wellies or a pair of glamorous high heels? Why not give her pretty painted toenails and a dainty toe-ring?

Hairstyle Hints

You can give Mandy any hair colour you like! Will you make her a redhead or a brunette? Perhaps you'll give her jet black hair with brightly coloured streaks — the choice is yours. You could even add cute bows to the end of her plaits to finish the look.

Add Accessories

Don't forget to design some funky accessories to match Mandy's new outfit. You could draw bangles, maybe a necklace or two, a bag, umbrella, earrings, a hair band... the possibilities are endless!

Draw your
designer outfit
here!

19

How To Draw A Bunny

Create this adorable rabbit in four easy steps...

1 Sketch your drawing in faint pencil first. Begin by giving your bunny two long ears and a round head. Draw another circular shape with a flat bottom to create the body.

2 Draw in your bunny's two front legs — one leg should have three toes and the other should have two. Add a small circle for the fluffy tail.

3 Draw over your final pencil lines in a fine black pen, rubbing out any stray pencil lines. Draw the nose and a 'w' shape underneath for the mouth. Add the bunny's eyes, eyebrows and whiskers to finish the face.

4 Use your pens, colouring pencils or crayons to colour in your bunny. Remember to give it a cute pink nose!

Tip: You can draw lots of bunnies with different coats — black, white, or even patchy!

20

Draw your bunny here!

Cookie's
Colour
and Design

Cookie loves to draw and colour. Fill this page with a rainbow of colour and design. Why not add some glitter, gems or sparkle too?

felt tips

22

My How To Draw Art File

How To Draw Gemma

1 Start by drawing an upside—down horseshoe shape for Gemma's hairline. Sketch in two rounded ears and the outline of her face. Add in her neck and shoulders.

2 Draw two straight lines on her body to give her arms. Add lots of curved lines all around Gemma's head for her hair and draw in four lines for her fringe.

3 Give Gemma a nice big smile and a pointy little nose. Draw in her eyebrows, just below her fringe, and give her two dots for eyes. Finally, add straight lines to her top to create stripes.

4 Time to colour in! Gemma has light brown hair and an orange and blue striped top.

24

Tip: Gemma misses Alice when she moves away — try giving her a sad facial expression.

Draw Gemma here!

You could become the next Nick Sharratt!

Art Equipment

Which materials will you use?

PENS

There are lots of different kinds of coloured pens but felt pens are probably the best for colouring in.

felt tips

Artist Tip!
Dip a dried—up felt pen in a little warm water to bring it magically to life!

PENCILS

Coloured pencils are good for colouring in smaller areas because of their small points.

Artist Tip!
Keep your coloured pencils upright in a clean container rather than a pencil case. This keeps the points nice and sharp.

CHALK

Coloured chalks can be messy but they're great for blending colours on paper. You can use a piece of tissue to smudge the colours together.

Artist Tip!
Spray your finished chalk drawing with a light layer of hairspray to fix the colours in place.

PAINT

Paints are perfect for colouring in large areas and there are lots of different kinds of paints to choose from:
• Poster paints are great for creating bright and bold pictures, like posters or cards, or painting Papier Mache projects.
• Watercolours are fun to use, too — just add water to your brush before dipping in the paint. The more water you add, the lighter the paint will become. Try using pale blue watercolour paint for a wishy—washy summer's day sky.

poster paints

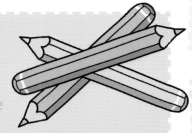

SKETCHBOOK

Every artist needs a sketchbook! You can use any size sketchbook you like but it's worthwhile keeping a small one in your bag — perfect if you spot something interesting to sketch while you're out and about!

Light And Shade

How to add light and shade to your drawing.

Take a look at this box.

The arrow shows which direction the light source is coming from. You can see that the light would hit the top of the box, but the front of the box would be in the shade. The artist has used a lighter shade to show where the light is hitting the surface and a darker shade to show the areas where the light can't reach.

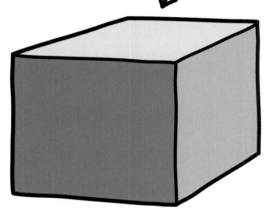

Now you try!

Artist Tip!
Adding light and shade to your drawing creates a realistic 3D effect.

Look at this apple.

You can see a round white spot in the top left corner. This arty trick makes the apple look round and shiny. Artists will often add white light spots to rounded objects to get the same 3D effect.

Why don't you try?

Artist Tip!

Look for shiny or reflective objects around the house — a kettle, vase or piece of fruit are all great items to draw. Use your new colouring techniques to add light and shade to your drawings to create mini masterpieces!

Top Techniques

Create super sketches with these top tips!

Rough Sketch

Often, an artist will do a rough sketch before finalising their drawing. This means they sketch a first drawing in pencil without worrying about mistakes or lines. Look at this rough sketch. Can you see how the drawing is quite messy and scratchy?

Now look at the finished drawing. The artist has rubbed out any stray lines before outlining his drawing and colouring it in

Cross-Hatch Shading

Look at this illustration from Lola Rose. Can you see how the lines criss—cross in sections? This technique is called cross—hatching. Cross—hatching is a great way to make areas on your drawing look darker. You can use a sharp pencil or fine black pen to draw lots of straight lines. Then simply draw more straight lines running in the opposite direction to create the criss—cross effect. Have a go at cross hatching in this box

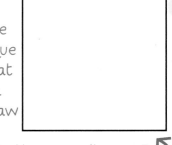

Artist Tip!

Never use a ruler for cross—hatching. A hand—drawn line looks more natural.

Movement

Ever wondered how to make something on paper look like it was moving? An easy way to do this is to draw curved lines around the object. Look at this drawing of a kangaroo. See how the kangaroo looks like it's bouncing around? Try adding your own movement lines to this dog

My Best Friends File

Fab stuff for you and your besties!

What's Inside-

Fun, giggles and games!

Best Friends

File

Puzzles & Games

Make & Create

A-Z of Best Friends

The fabulous things about friendships!

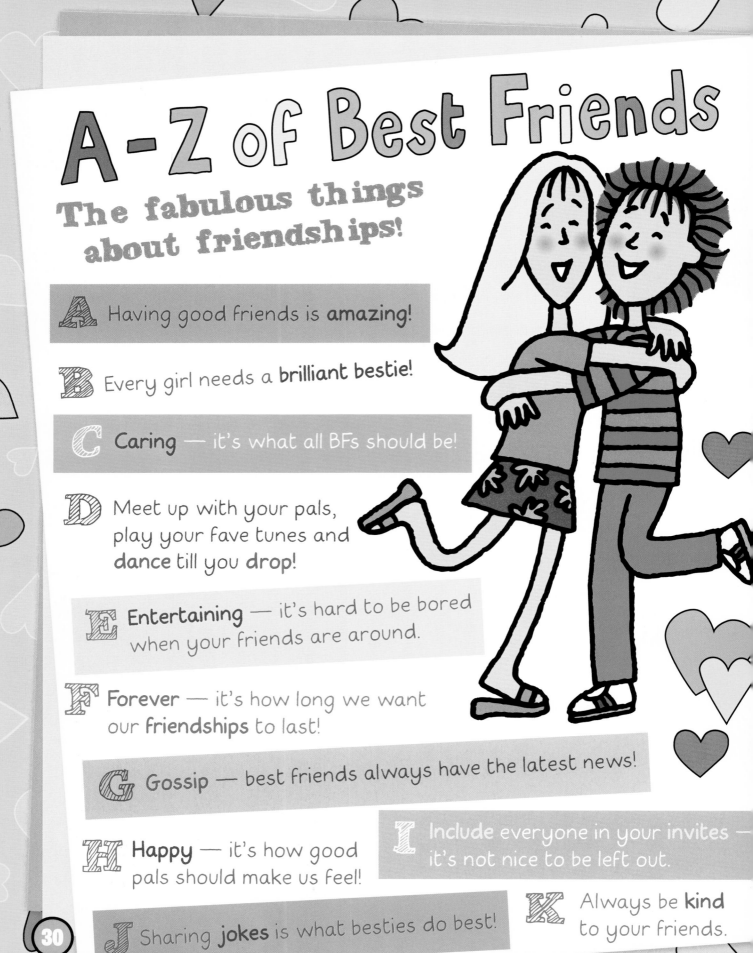

A Having good friends is **amazing!**

B Every girl needs a **brilliant bestie!**

C Caring — it's what all BFs should be!

D Meet up with your pals, play your fave tunes and **dance** till you **drop!**

E Entertaining — it's hard to be bored when your friends are around.

F Forever — it's how long we want our **friendships** to last!

G Gossip — best friends always have the latest news!

H Happy — it's how good pals should make us feel!

I Include everyone in your invites — it's not nice to be left out.

J Sharing **jokes** is what besties do best!

K Always be **kind** to your friends.

 My Best Friends File

L You'll never be **lonely** with a BFF. Friends can always make you **LOL**!

M **Mean** — something a friend should never be!

N It's cool to have old friends but great to make **new** ones too!

O **Outfits** — your bestie can help you choose the best look for any occasion.

P Friends are always there to share your **problems**.

Q **Quarrels** — try to sort out any arguments and not let them drag on too long.

R **Rock** out to your favourite songs together, singing into your hairbrushes!

S **Sharing**, **secrets** and **shopping** — it's what best friends are for!

T You can always **trust** a best friend. She'll keep your secrets safe forever.

U Your bestie will always **understand** if you feel **unhappy**.

V **Valuable** — a great BF is worth a million!

W **Weekends** — the best time to get together and have fun!

X **X-tra** special — send your friend a note, text or email to say how special she is.

Y **Yap** till you **yawn** with your BFF!

Z **Zzzz** — sleepovers with your best buddies are awesome!

What's Your Best Friend DESTINY?

Match your star sign with your bestie's and discover what the symbol says about your friendship!

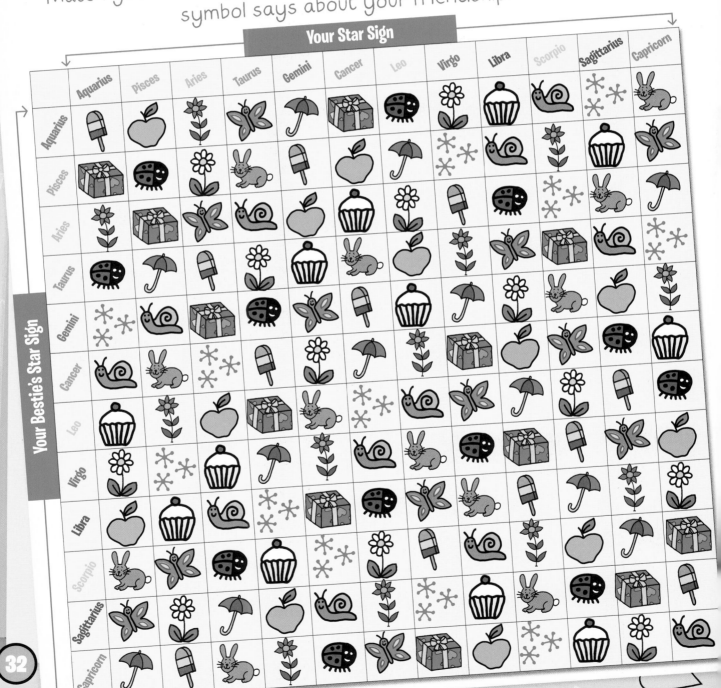

Now you can see what your symbol means for your friendship!

My Best Friends File

Present — Make time to do something creative with your friend, like making matching bracelets.

Butterfly — Sometimes you argue, but it's only because you're like sisters.

Umbrella — you two are so close that you don't go a day without talking!

Ladybird — You both enjoy different hobbies, but reading is the thing that keeps you together.

Rabbit — she's always making jokes and you're always giggling — you're the perfect match!

Snail — She's like your good luck charm — life isn't as fun when she's not there!

White flower — There's nothing you like more than spending time together and baking tasty treats.

Apple — You're connected by how caring you are and your love for animals.

Purple flower — You love gossiping, although you can both keep secrets when you really need to!

Cupcake — Just because you don't talk all the time doesn't mean you're not good friends.

Ice lolly — She's loud and you're shy, but it doesn't mean you can't be friends. Opposites attract!

Snowflakes — The two of you share an amazing secret that no one else knows!

Best Friend Blushes

Red Face Ratings

★ ★ ★   So shameful!

★ ★ ★ ★   No Way!

★ ★ ★ ★ ★   Major Blush

Monkey Business

I spent ages making a pretty birthday card with a kitten on it for my bestie's birthday. I'd just put it in the envelope when I remembered that my annoying brother's birthday was on the same day. I quickly scribbled another card with a hairy monkey on the cover and stuck it in another envelope. I couldn't believe it when my friend opened her card on her birthday and pulled out the card with a hairy monkey on it — I'd mixed up the birthday cards!

Kayleigh, Perth

Rating: ★ ★ ★ ★ ★

Soggy Sandwiches

I was sitting in the lunch hall with my best friend and we were pretending to be pop stars. She was singing into a banana and I was using my bottle of fizzy lemonade as a microphone. All of a sudden the bottle top shot off and lemonade fizzed all over my bestie — and her sandwiches! She wasn't impressed!

Cerys, Bradford

Rating: ★ ★ ★ ★ ★

Lost Property

My best friend got a really cute charm bracelet for her birthday and I was over the moon when she said I could borrow it to wear to my Nana's party. I was horrified when, after the party, I realised I'd lost it! I searched *everywhere* for it but it was nowhere to be seen. My mum was really cross with me because she had to buy a replacement bracelet for my friend!

Lexi, Chester

Rating: ★☆☆☆☆

Dance Disaster

I was at my bestie's house one Saturday showing off a really tricky dance routine in front of her mum and sisters. I got really into it and threw my arms about a bit too much, accidentally knocking her mum's favourite china lady off the mantelpiece! It fell to the floor and broke into lots of pieces. I was so embarrassed!

Jenny, Swansea

Rating: ★★★★★

My Best Friends File

Bus Bump!

I was sitting beside my best friend on the bus on a school trip. We were mucking about when she started tickling me. I'm really ticklish and I was squirming and laughing so hard I fell right off my seat and bumped on my bum in the middle of the bus! Everyone laughed at me and my teacher made me come and sit beside her. Oh, the shame!

Bella, Romford

Rating: ★★★★★

Cake-astrophe!

My bestie arrived for a sleepover with a big box of cakes she'd made for our midnight feast. Later, we were all snuggled up in our pyjamas and started tucking in. I took a bite of one of her cakes — it tasted disgusting! I had to run to the bathroom to be sick and when I got back she didn't look very happy with me! Ooops!

Rainie, Isle of Man

Rating: ★★★★★

Rainbow Personality Revealer

My favourite food is this colour

This colour makes me happy

The cover of my favourite book is...

My favourite cartoon character is...

The colour of my school bag is...

My bedroom is painted...

RED ☑
You are bouncy, funny and chatty! Your jokes always make your friends laugh.

ORANGE ☑
You are curious about everything! You love learning and school is lots of fun

YELLOW ☑
You love animals and hugs. You like spending time with your special bestie.

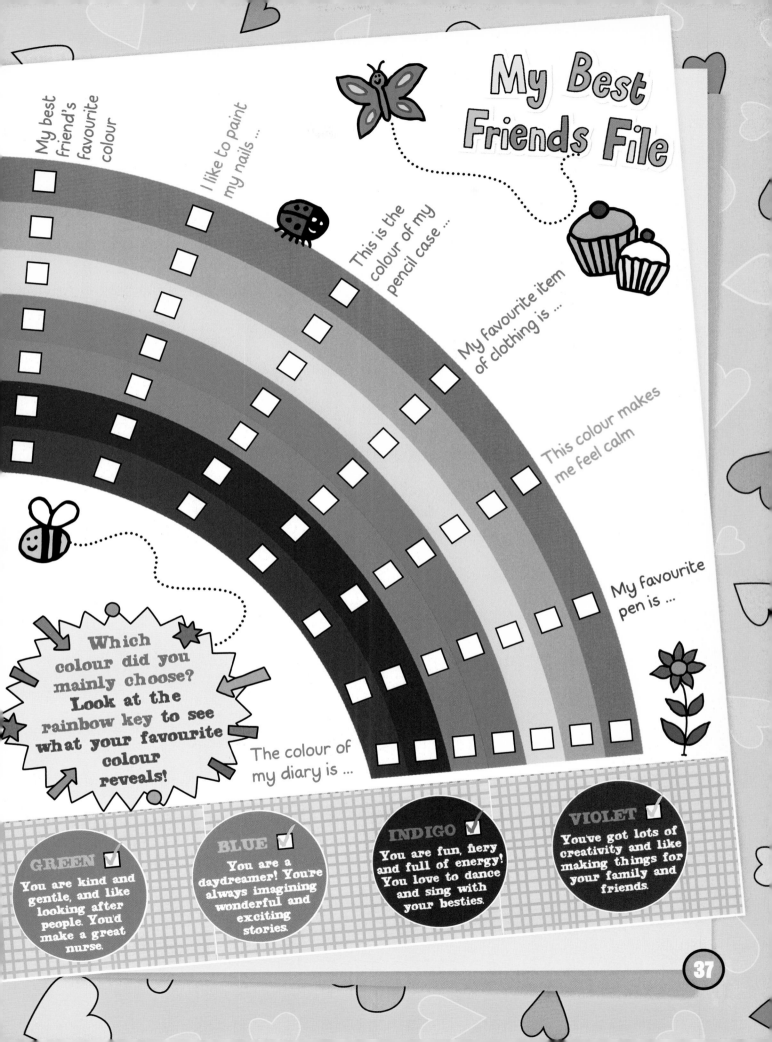

My Best Friends File

My best friend's favourite colour

I like to paint my nails ...

This is the colour of my pencil case ...

My favourite item of clothing is ...

This colour makes me feel calm

My favourite pen is ...

Which colour did you mainly choose? Look at the rainbow key to see what your favourite colour reveals!

The colour of my diary is ...

GREEN ✓
You are kind and gentle, and like looking after people. You'd make a great nurse.

BLUE ✓
You are a daydreamer! You're always imagining wonderful and exciting stories.

INDIGO ✓
You are fun, fiery and full of energy! You love to dance and sing with your besties.

VIOLET ✓
You've got lots of creativity and like making things for your family and friends.

Super-fun Sleepover!

Ten awesome ideas for the best sleepover **ever**!

1. Tracy Beaker's Ball of Truth

You'll need an inflatable beach ball and a permanent marker pen. Before your sleepover starts, blow up the ball and write fun questions all over it.

You can ask questions like:

What do you say when you talk in your sleep?

What are you really, really scared of?

If you were invisible what would you do?

If you were an animal what would you be?

What three words would you use to describe yourself?

Think of things you would want to know about others. The more questions you can fit on the ball, the better!

Place everyone in a circle and throw the ball to someone. The person who catches the ball must answer the question that's closest to their **right** thumb. Keep throwing and answering to reveal everyone's secrets!

2. Drama Queens

Split into two teams and go into different rooms.

Each team gets a bag filled with five random, mystery items. For example — a toothbrush, doughnut, flip-flops, teabag and mop.

Each team has 15 minutes to make up a funny story or mini-play using all five items.

Now it's time for the teams to perform their silly stories for each other.

3. Terrible Talents

Instead of impressing your BFs with your best talent, you have to show off your worst. So if your singing is lame you have to share your karaoke shame. If your dancing is pants, it's time to perform your worst routine.

4. Mad Makeovers

You'll need a blindfold or slumber mask and a selection of makeup.

The first person puts on the blindfold and does the makeup of the second person.

When they're done, the second person puts on the blindfold and makes up the third person.

Keep going until everyone's had a mad makeover — take plenty of pictures of your crazy results!

39

5. Silly Songs

Up to six people can play this game. You'll need two dice.

Give each person a number and roll the dice.

The number on the first dice is the singer, the number on the second dice is the song picker.

The song picker has to make up a song title. It can be anything they like, for example – I Like Cuddling Fluffy Kittens.

The singer has to make up a silly song to fit the title.

6. I Want My Mummy!

You'll need 4–6 rolls of white toilet paper.

⭐ Split into two teams and give each team some toilet paper.

⭐ One person from each team has to be the mummy.

⭐ Start the clock and see which team is first to wrap their mummy from head to toe in toilet paper bandages.

⭐ Give extra marks for neatness!

7. Ssssshhhh!

Use any toilet paper left from the mummy game.

Pass the roll around asking each person to tear off as much as they think they'll need for the game.

Don't tell anyone what the game is about until they've all taken their paper.

Now you reveal that they have to share a secret for each square of paper they have!

8. Spooky Sweetie Hunt

You'll need small choccy bars and torches.

Before everyone arrives at the party ask a parent to hide the sweets around the house.

Watch out for spooky shadows!

chocolate bar

Now turn off all the lights and search for the sweets using only the torches.

Tip: It's fun to play this in the garden if the weather's fine.

My Best Friends File

jelly spider

yum!

9. Candy Changeover

sweeties

yum!

You'll need two small bowls, a straw and 20 small sweets (like M&Ms) for each player.

- Give each person an empty bowl and a bowl full of sweets.
- You have to move the sweets from one bowl to the other by sucking them on to the end of the straw — no hands allowed.
- Winner is the one who finishes first.

10. Pass The Polish

This is just like pass the parcel but you pass round a bottle of nail polish instead.

When the music stops the person with the polish has to paint as many nails as possible.

Start the music again and pass the polish.

Winner is the first to paint all finger and toe nails.

Tip: Video some of your games and performances for LOL later!

Sort My Sleepover

Use this handy list for all your sleepover must-haves. Check it off as you arrange each thing.

Invites

- ☐ **Made/Bought**
- ☐ **Written**
- ☐ **Sent**

Food

- ☐ **Crisps**
- ☐ **Cookies**
- ☐ **Pizza**
- ☐ **Popcorn**
- ☐ **Milkshakes**
- ☐ **Cupcakes**
- ☐ **Fruit**
- ☐ **Hot chocolate**

Games and Entertainment

- ☐ **Music**
- ☐ **DVDs**
- ☐ **Toilet paper**
- ☐ **Beach ball**
- ☐ **Blindfold**
- ☐ **Straws**
- ☐ **Dice**
- ☐ **Torches**
- ☐ **Sweets**
- ☐ **Prizes for winners**

My STORY SCHOOL File

How to write like Jacky!

What's Inside—

You could be the next best-selling author!

zoom!

Alice and Gemma

felt tips

icecream

File
STORY SCHOOL

Puzzles & Games

Make & Create

My Writing Secrets

Write a story with me!

When I was young I loved a famous book called *Little Women*. The story was about four very different sisters. Meg was the eldest, and she was very good and sensible. My favourite sister was Jo, who was full of fun, a very untidy tomboy who loved writing. Then there was shy Beth who was musical and devoted to her dolls. The youngest sister was Amy, who was artistic and pretty and a little bit vain.

Shall we make up a story together about four sisters? I've done this already in *The Diamond Girls*, but I'm going to make up new girls today.

Okay, think of four names. My girls are going to be called Queenie, Lulu, Natasha and Cherry.

Write your girls' names here:

- - - - - - - - - - - - - - - - -

- - - - - - - - - - - - - - - - -

- - - - - - - - - - - - - - - - -

- - - - - - - - - - - - - - - - -

I think Queenie is 14, Lulu is 12, Natasha is 10 and Cherry is 7. How old are your girls? Write their ages beside their names.

Queenie is very pretty, with long fair hair. She's terribly bossy too, and always wants her own way — but she tries hard to look after her sisters. Lulu is plain and dreamy and loves reading. Natasha calls herself Nat, and is a real tomboy, and brilliant at gymnastics. Cherry is very funny, loves dancing, and wears cherry bobbles in her hair. What are your girls like? Describe them here.

My girls are quite poor now — their dad has lost his job. Are your girls part of a poor family too? Are they incredibly rich, with celebrity parents? Are they orphans, living with a strict aunt? Write a little story about their family here.

Now, something's got to happen in our story! I think my girls are all going to try hard to find some way of making money to help their parents. Queenie might start delivering the local newspaper (and maybe she'll meet an interesting boy on her round!). Lulu will go along to an old people's home and read aloud to everyone, though she'll be very shy at first. Natasha will demonstrate sports equipment at the local shopping centre. Cherry will win a dancing competition — and get a part in a television show!

There! It's your turn now. Jot down what's going to happen to your girls. I'd love to read some of your completed stories.

----

vroom!

What Happened Next?

Ever wished you could find out what happens to your favourite characters? Have fun writing your **own** endings!

Cookie

Where the book left off:

Beauty and her mum are happily living with their good friend Mike in a little cottage by the sea. Then all of Beauty's dreams come true when she appears on a TV show and meets her idol Sam and his bunny, Lily.

What do you think happens next?

_____

_____

_____

_____

Things to think about:
★ Will Dilly marry Mike?
★ What will Beauty call her new baby bunny?
★ What will become of Beauty's mean dad?

My Sister Jodie

Where the book left off:

A terrible tragedy has turned poor Pearl's life upside down. Things will never be the same, but a surprise addition to the family could change everything...

What do you think happens next?

_____

_____

_____

Things to think about:
★ Will baby May grow up to be just like Jodie?
★ How will shy Pearl get on at her new school?
★ Will Pearl ever go back to Melchester College?

STORY SCHOOL

Candyfloss

What do you think happens next?

Where the book left off:

It's the summer holidays and Floss and her dad have decided to join the fair — Dad will help out on the fairground rides, Floss will sell candyfloss, and they will all live together in Rose's cosy caravan.

Things to think about:

★ Will Dad let Floss dye her hair pink?

★ Will Mum decide to stay in Australia for good?

★ Can Rose teach Floss how to read palms?

Clean Break

What do you think happens next?

Where the book left off:

It's Christmas Eve and Em and her family are sad — Gran is in Spain with her new boyfriend, Eddie, and Dad hasn't come to visit. The family are just getting into bed when someone starts knocking at the door...

Things to think about:

★ Who do you think is knocking on the door?

★ Will Gran decide to stay in Spain with Eddie?

★ Will Em's family ever be whole again?

vroom!

47

Start Your Own Book Club!

Invite your friends!

Who would you like to ask to join your book group? Pick a handful of friends — a small group usually works best. You could make your own book club invites and special membership cards for each of your friends.

Jot down the names of your book club members here:

....
....
....
....
....

Choose a name

Think of a name for your book club. You could be The Bookworms, The Bookends, Story Stars, Jacky's Readers — anything you like!

Write the name of your book club here:

....

Meeting place

The fairest way is to each take it in turns to hold the book club at one another's houses. If you can't have it at home, ask your teacher if you can hold a meeting in the school at break time. Why not ask each book club member to bring along a snack for a book club feast — yum!

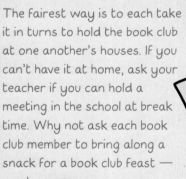

Pick a book!

One person will pick a book and everyone will read it. Remember, each book club member will read at a different speed so make sure to leave three or four weeks before you next meet up to discuss the book.

The first book we will read is:

....

Discussion time

Time for the fun part! One person should lead the group and start the discussion. The rest of the group can then take it in turns to share their opinion.

You can talk about absolutely anything you like. If you find you are stuck for ideas, try the topic starter.

The leader for our first meeting is:

....

Short and sweet

You don't want anyone to get bored so try to keep your meetings short and make sure each member gets the chance to have their say.

Make notes

Keep a notebook especially for book club meetings.

Jot down the title and author of the chosen book at the top of the page. You could even include a short summary of the story if you like. Each member can then write their opinion in the book club notebook and rate the book out of five.

Have fun!

Copy these stars into your book club notebook. You can colour them in to rate your book out of five!

Hot Topics!

Struggling to get started? Roll a dice and find the perfect question to start the discussion!

1 What did you like about the main character? Is there anything you didn't like?

2 Did you like the ending?

3 Which character did you like least? Why do you think that is?

4 What was your favourite part of the story?

5 What would you change about the story?

6 Do you think you are like any of the characters in the book?

vroom!

Create A Goodie!

All you need to know about creating a good character for a story!

★ Show your character's bravery. Maybe they have to do something they've never done before, or they have a friend who needs help.

★ Write a scene or two from the good character's point of view. Does he or she understand the bad character and want to help him?

★ What's your character's best friend like? Are they a joker always making people laugh? Maybe they're someone who always has good advice? Draw a rough picture of them here:

★ Give your character a stand—out feature. This could be anything from having a phrase they say all the time to winding their hair around their finger when they're nervous.

★ Remember that no person is perfect, so even though your character is good they still need to have flaws.

★ Come up with a name for your character, but only after you have developed their personality. Write your ideas here:

Create A Baddie!

Now you can use these tips to create a naughty character!

STORY SCHOOL

The Daily

★ Decide how evil your character is going to be. Are they trying to take over the world or are they a bit of a bully?

★ What sort of relationship does your baddie have with their family? Do they speak to them at all?

★ A bad character isn't bad for no reason. Give your character a background that explains their actions. If you don't want to tell the whole story you can give little hints.

★ Remember, no one thinks of themselves as evil. Your character must see everyone else as the people with problems, not themself.

★ Think about what your bad character is called — a villain sometimes has a "bad" sounding name.
Write down a few names in the box below:

★ Does your bad character have any friends? Or do people just talk to them because they're scared of them? Make a list of the things people could be scared of:

★ Decide if your baddie has a turning point and realises their mistakes, or if they stay a bad character until the end of the story.

vroom!

Alice and Gemma

Story Starter

Stuck for a story idea? Get started here...

Magic Numbers

Use your name to create a character name.

- Add the numbers for your initials together, for example
  Tracy Beaker (T + B) is 7 + 1 = 8
- If your number is 10 or more, add the digits together until you get a number between 1 and 9, for example **10: 1 + 0 = 1**
- Now choose the name that matches your number

Use names of friends and family to create more characters

1 = ABC	4 = JKL	7 = STU
2 = DEF	5 = MNO	8 = VWX
3 = GHI	6 = PQR	9 = YZ

1. Antonia Pepperoni
2. Stella Starchild
3. Maximus Presley
4. Mimi Moonglow
5. Precious Skye
6. Krystal Oceana
7. Charlie McCloud
8. Betsy Beiber
9. Donatella De Vine

Pick A Personality!

Heads- naughty
Tails- swotty

Heads- happy
Tails- lonely

Heads- kind
Tails- spiteful

Heads- glamorous
Tails- plain

Birthday Match

Use the month you were born to choose an outstanding feature for your character.

January - Hair that's long enough to sit on

February - Two different colour eyes

March - Long nails painted with fantastic designs

April - Wild curls like Tracy Beaker's

May - Unfashionable clothes

June - Terrified of water

July - A funny laugh that sounds like a donkey

August - Uses a wheelchair

September - Doesn't speak — just like Lizzie Zipmouth

October - Has a very noticeable birth mark

November - Cries very easily

December - Can't read but tries to keep it a secret

STORY SCHOOL

Think carefully about how the feature affects your character and work it into your story. For example -

Are they bullied because of it?

Does it stop them from doing things?

Do other people think they are weird?

Does it make them miserable?

Do they feel special because of it?

Flip a coin to choose personality traits from each section

Heads - chatty
Tails - quiet

Heads - funny
Tails - annoying

Heads - rich
Tails - poor

Heads - lucky
Tails - unlucky

Turn over for more!

vroom!

Favourites Finder

Roll a dice to pick favourite things for your character.

FOOD

1	2	3	4	5	6
CHIPS	CABBAGE	CHOCCY	SPAGHETTI	BANANAS	FISH

SHOES

1	2	3	4	5	6
TRAINERS	BOOTS	SLIPPERS	SPARKLY BALLET PUMPS	FLIP-FLOPS	HIGH HEELS

ACTIVITY

1	2	3	4	5	6
WRITING	DRAWING	BAKING	SWIMMING	GYMNASTICS	DANCING

COLOUR

1	2	3	4	5	6
RED	PINK	BLUE	BLACK	GREEN	ORANGE

STYLE

1	2	3	4	5	6
GIRLIE	TOMBOY	ROCK CHICK	FASHION FABULOUS	OLD FASHIONED	BABYISH

TREASURED POSSESSION

1	2	3	4	5	6
AN OLD BABY BLANKET	A CHARM BRACELET	A PHOTO OF THEIR FAMILY	POSTCARD FROM OLDEN TIMES	A BLUE LACE HANKIE	A JEWELLED BOX

What's Your Story Setting?

This magic square will help you pick!

What to do:
- Pick a number between 1 and 4.
- Pick a JW character.
- Pick another character and look under the flap to find your story setting.
- Open and close the square the same number of times.
- Open and close again as you spell out their name.

How to make it:

1. Cut out the square and turn it over so this side is face down.

2. Fold each corner into the centre to make a smaller square. 3. Turn it back over, fold the corners into the centre again then fold the square in half. 4. Put a thumb and index finger under each numbered flap and push the four corners together to meet in the middle.

1

2

3

4

Tracy

Jodie

Ella

Cookie

Henry

Chloe

Sunset

Biscuits

Your character is a fabulous and extremely famous Hollywood movie star living in a humungous designer house. Is life really that brilliant? You decide!

Your character is being held captive in a locked tower in a spooky haunted mansion. Could there be a secret passage hidden somewhere in the room...

Your character finds an abandoned dog and longs to keep it. But things become very complicated as the two friends try to stay together.

Your character creates a special project and it could win a competition. But it has to be presented to a big crowd to decide the winner. Can they do it?

Your character lives in Victorian times and something happens to change their life completely. Will there be a happy ending — or not?

Your character is invited to a super-glam and star studded party. Who will be there? What will your character wear? Will the party be as good as it seems?

Your character invents something amazing but lots of people are trying to steal the idea for themselves. Will you character win out or be cheated?

Your character is soppy and bullied at school by a gang of mean girls. What can your character do to change this situation?

Now you've created a character and picked a story setting so get writing!
Try to work in all your results for an interesting and exciting tale.

vroom!

55

How to Write a Haiku

Just like Andy from *The Suitcase Kid*

What is a Haiku?

Haikus are little Japanese poems. They're simple and very good for describing things like moments, wishes or seasons. They normally don't rhyme.

Traditional rules for writing Haikus meant they had to be three lines long with five syllables in the first line, seven in the next and five in the last. These days you can write three or four lines, but no more than 17 syllables in each poem.

What is a syllable?

This is how many sounds you have to make to say a word. Think about how you say things and count the syllables —

For example:

sy—lla—ble
Hai—ku
So *syllable* has three syllables and *Haiku* has two. Clap while you speak to help you count.

Write your own Haiku

Jot down what you want to say or describe —

For example:

My gorgeous and fluffy kitten, he loves playing with his toys or running in the garden. He loves the warm sunshine.

Now think of how you can cut this down and turn it into a Haiku. The first one below has exactly 17 syllables and follows the traditional rules —

1 So furry and cute
He runs and plays in the sun
My lovely kitten

Or follow the modern rules like this

2 My sweet, soft kitten
Fluffy and cute
Loves to run and play
In the sun

Now you try - once you start you won't be able to stop!

56

My Puzzles & Games File

Champion Tracy

Will you be puzzle champion?

What's Inside-

Get busy with the quizzes!

Puzzles & Games

Make & Create

FIND YOUR DIAMOND

You're a happy friendly person who loves to chatter away with friends, just like Dixie! You both love animals and dream of having a pet of your very own. Dixie desperately wants a budgie – what's YOUR favourite pet?

DIXIE

GO BLONDE

Martine likes to stand out from the crowd with her dyed blonde hair and cool hairstyles. She's also pretty stubborn at times, just like you, but you're also loyal and loving – friends know they can trust you with their biggest secrets.

MARTINE

I have a
wild
imagination — NO

I do talk
a LOT! ← YES

NO — My fashion
style is
totally
unique

START — YES

I make
friends
easily

NO

YES — I'd love a
pet
budgie

NO — I'm great
at keeping
secrets

YES

YES — Stubborn?
Me?!

NO — I spend ages
getting
ready for
school

YES

NO

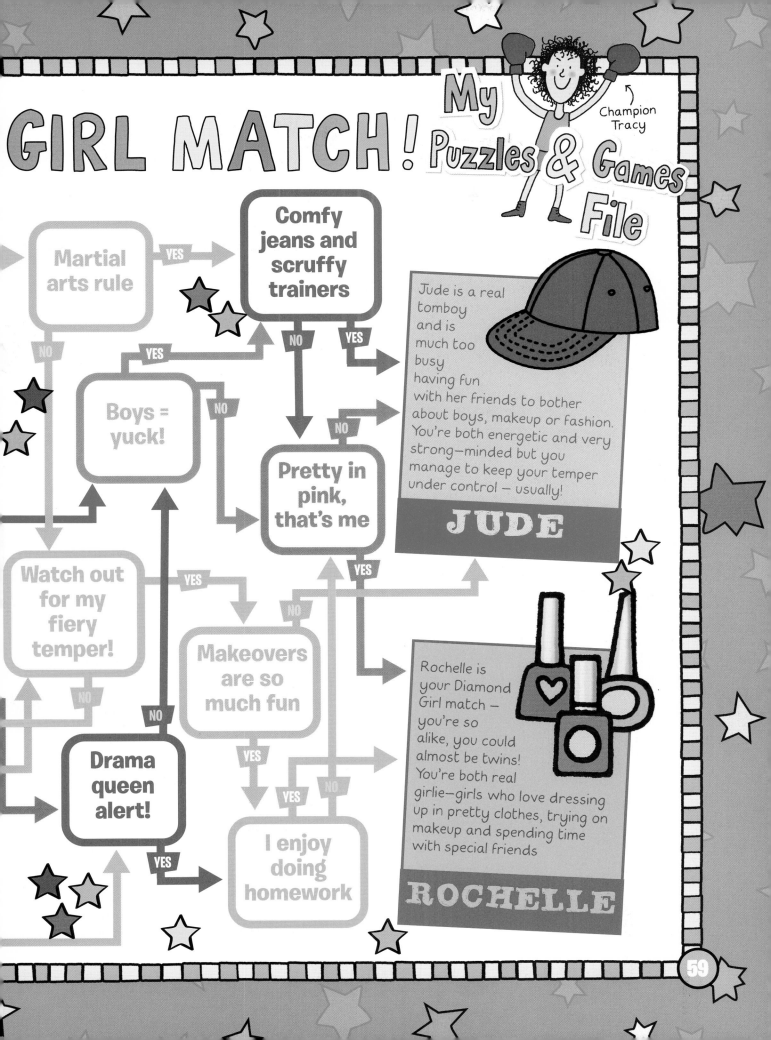

GIRL MATCH!

Champion Tracy

Martial arts rule — YES → **Comfy jeans and scruffy trainers**

NO

YES → **Boys = yuck!**

NO

Pretty in pink, that's me

Watch out for my fiery temper! — YES

NO

Makeovers are so much fun

Drama queen alert! — YES

I enjoy doing homework

Jude is a real tomboy and is much too busy having fun with her friends to bother about boys, makeup or fashion. You're both energetic and very strong—minded but you manage to keep your temper under control — usually!

JUDE

Rochelle is your Diamond Girl match — you're so alike, you could almost be twins! You're both real girlie—girls who love dressing up in pretty clothes, trying on makeup and spending time with special friends

ROCHELLE

59

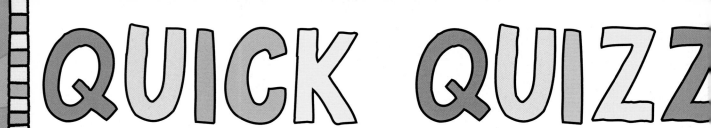

Are You A Drama Queen?

2. Your little sister has broken your favourite pen. So you...

C. Tell her it's okay — you know she didn't mean to

A. Let out a scream and throw yourself to the ground in distress

B. Give her a good telling off and storm off in a huff

1. Your favourite song comes on the radio. You:

C. Hum along quietly and tap your feet

B. Sing loudly and try out a few funky dance moves

A. Perform a spectacular pop show on the kitchen table

3. You decide to audition for the part of Dorothy in the school's production of *The Wizard of Oz*. You:

B. Watch the film over and over again until you know it off by heart

C. Practise your lines every day with your bestie

A. Start wearing ruby red slippers to school and rename your dog Toto

4. It's your birthday! Your birthday cake is:

C. Pale pink with Happy Birthday written in icing

B. A special photograph cake of yourself

A. Four different flavour tiers with hundreds of candles on top

5. Mum has forgotten to record *Tracy Beaker Returns!* You say:

A. 'That's it! I'm moving out right NOW!'

C. 'Don't worry, Mum. I'll watch the repeat some other time'

B. 'I'm devastated — I was soooo looking forward to watching that'

Mostly A	**Mostly B**	**Mostly C**
DRAMA QUEEN DIVA	STAR PERFORMER	SPOTLIGHT SHY
You're totally over–the–top, *dahling!*	You love to be the centre of attention.	You're not one to cause a fuss.

Tracy's Cringe Challenge!

Would you rather...

Which of these cringing choices will you pick?

ES

Fun quizzes for you and your besties!

Champion Tracy

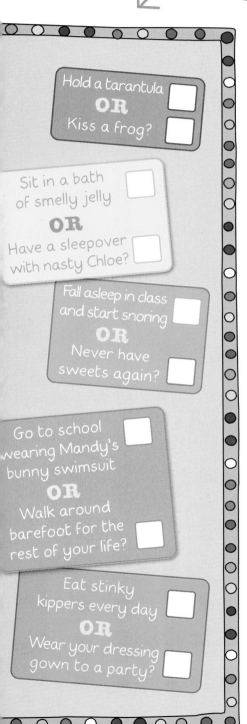

Hold a tarantula
OR
Kiss a frog?

Sit in a bath of smelly jelly
OR
Have a sleepover with nasty Chloe?

Fall asleep in class and start snoring
OR
Never have sweets again?

Go to school wearing Mandy's bunny swimsuit
OR
Walk around barefoot for the rest of your life?

Eat stinky kippers every day
OR
Wear your dressing gown to a party?

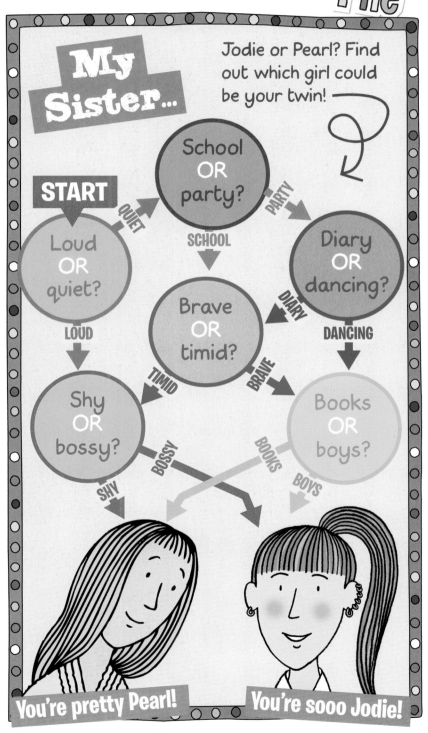

My Sister...

Jodie or Pearl? Find out which girl could be your twin!

START

School OR party?

QUIET

PARTY

SCHOOL

Loud OR quiet?

Diary OR dancing?

LOUD

Brave OR timid?

DIARY

DANCING

TIMID

BRAVE

Shy OR bossy?

Books OR boys?

BOSSY

BOOKS

SHY

BOYS

You're pretty Pearl!

You're sooo Jodie!

61

Destiny's Dares

LOL with this fun game!

You'll need a pencil and a CD of party tunes to play.

What to do:

1. Stick this page to card and cut out the spinner. Ask an adult to push a pencil through the centre.
2. Cut out the dares and put them in a bowl.
3. Write out the CD song names on some paper strips and put these in another bowl.

How to play:

1. Pass round the bowl of CD song titles for everyone to pick. Keep passing till all the titles are finished
2. Play the CD on random shuffle. If your song comes on, stop the music and pick a dare from the bowl.
3. Spin the dare wheel. It will tell you to take the dare or pass it to a friend.

Make up some of your own dares too.

Put pants on your head, socks on your hands and dance to your fave song.

Eat a biscuit spread with toothpaste. Yuk!

Name 10 JW books in a minute or less.

Yawn till you make someone else yawn.

Ew! Eat a sweet covered with tomato sauce and squeezy cheese.

Pretend to be a monkey or an elephant — in the garden!

Name 10 JW characters in a minute or less.

Wear your mum's coat and some big wellies and walk to the end of the street.

Reveal a secret or tell a cringing story about yourself.

Do an impression of your favourite pop star.

Answer every question you're asked with the word 'no' for the next 30 minutes.

Answer every question you're asked with the word yes for the next 30 minutes.

Limbo dance under a broom handle.

Do a cheesy action dance — like Agadoo, The Birdie Song or the Court of King Caractacus. Cringing!

Lie upside down, draw a face on your chin with eye pencil and sing a song.

Put on your most frumpy outfit and your slippers and wear them till the game's over.

Stand outside and sing a song really loudly.

Ask your BF to put some lipgloss on you — with her eyes shut!

Drink a glass of cola mixed with cold tea, orange juice and a pinch of salt.

Hee-haw like a donkey and grunt like a pig.

Cluck like a chicken and bark like a dog.

Sniff a smelly shoe or sock. Gross!

Wear a sparkly tiara and fairy wings and perform a ballet dance in the garden.

Do an impression of Tracy Beaker having one of her worst ever tantrums!

Tracy's Wordsearch Challenge

Champion Tracy

Can you find the hidden words? Watch out — one of the words is NOT in the grid!

P	O	O	P	D	F	M	C	B	I	R	J	C	R	A
A	M	J	D	N	Z	O	I	O	O	U	N	A	E	D
Z	T	V	Z	U	X	W	S	K	S	C	L	S	C	O
V	U	T	B	O	M	L	I	T	E	D	U	C	C	P
Y	H	D	A	R	Y	N	I	K	E	O	K	Y	A	T
N	G	N	W	G	Y	N	H	N	H	R	S	R	M	I
N	N	W	H	G	E	F	P	E	U	I	I	J	S	O
E	A	W	H	N	J	E	E	W	O	D	G	N	M	N
J	U	A	W	I	A	R	S	N	I	F	G	L	G	R
J	I	S	Q	P	T	L	N	I	L	W	V	L	N	E
H	B	X	L	M	P	B	M	K	U	V	F	N	Y	S
N	A	L	L	U	G	Z	R	Q	P	O	E	P	N	G
R	X	E	K	D	P	E	T	E	R	L	L	Y	A	O
T	R	A	C	Y	B	E	A	K	E	R	R	K	N	V
T	S	D	P	W	L	E	N	I	A	L	E	A	Z	X

ADOPTION

ELAINE

JENNY

MIKE

TRACY BEAKER

CAM

ELM TREE HOUSE

CAMILLA

NOISY

DUMPING GROUND

FOSTERING

LOUISE

PETER

JUSTINE

SOLUTION

Missing Word: Camilla

The missing word is ....

Solve the JW Swirl!

Solve the clues and fill in the answers. They're all connected to Jacky's books and characters.

Elaine

1. Dixie, Rochelle, Jude and Martine are known as The _ _ _ _ _ _ _ _ _ _ _ _

6. A book about Destiny and Sunset

8. Tracy's nickname for her social worker

5. Jade's BF, Vicky _ _ _ _ _

4. Her favourite things are whales and Butterscotch

2. Dolphin's sister

3. A flower that goes with Lola

7. She's super-mean to Beauty

START

My Puzzles & Games File

Champion Tracy

The **last** letter of each answer is the **first** letter of the next.

12. Elsa's new BF

11. Floss's ex–best friend

Miss Brown

13. Treasure hides in —————'s attic

14. She's Lily —————

9. He does all the drawings for Jacky's books

10. Miss Brown is Tracy Beaker's —————

15. It's the worst Christmas **ever** when her dad leaves on Boxing Day morning!

END

ANSWERS 1. Diamond Girls 2. Star 3. Rose 4. Ella 5. Angel 6. Little Darlings 7. Skye 8. Elaine the Pain 9. Nick Sharratt 10. Teacher 11. Rhiannon 12. Naomi 13. India 14. Alone 15. Em

67

Sudoku
Starring Tracy Beaker!

Can you correctly fit Tracy and her friends (and enemies!) into the grid? Every row, column and mini-grid must contain one picture of each of them.

Justine

Cam

Elaine

Peter

Louise

ANSWERS
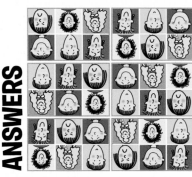

Take the JW Test!

Cut out and quiz your friends!

Take the JW Test!

Cut out and quiz your friends!

Cookie

1. What TV show does Beauty like to watch?
2. What does Beauty call the teddy she wins at Rhona's birthday party?
3. What stage show do the girls go to see on Beauty's birthday?
4. How does Mum pay for the mirror Beauty breaks?
5. What's the name of the guest house Beauty and Mum live in Rabbit Cove?
6. What does Mike give Beauty for her first day at her new school?

ANSWERS: 1. Rabbit Hutch 2. Nicholas Navybear 3. Birthday Bonanza 4. Sells her diamond necklace 5. Lily Cottage 6. Bright red baseball boots

---

Hetty FeatheR

1. What does Jem give Hetty for a good luck gift?
2. Who does Hetty think is her real mum?
3. What is Hetty's Foundling number?
4. Can you name all of Hetty's foster brothers and sisters? There are 10 of them!
5. What are the children celebrating when Hetty runs away?
6. What does Sissy sell?

ANSWERS: 1. A shiny silver sixpence 2. Madame Adeline 3. 25629 4. Jem, Gideon, Saul, Martha, Rosie, Nat, Eliza, Marcus, Bess and Nora 5. The Queen's Golden Jubilee 6. Flowers

---

Starring Tracy Beaker

1. What does Tracy tell everyone her mum does for a living?
2. What is Tracy's nickname for her social worker?
3. Who is Tracy's Number 1 enemy?
4. What part did Tracy get in the school production of A Christmas Carol?
5. Which teacher bans her from taking part?
6. What do Cam and Tracy have for Christmas dinner?

ANSWERS: 1. Hollywood movie star 2. Elaine the Pain 3. Justine Littlewood 4. Scrooge 5. Mrs Darlow 6. Egg and chips

---

Lily Alone

1. Who was Pixie's dad — Paul or Mikey?
2. What does Lily want to be when she grows up?
3. What animals do they see in the big park?
4. What did Lily use for counting in her pretend maths lesson?
5. Mr Abbot brought some postcards from the gallery to Lily. What were they pictures of?
6. Where does Lily take everyone to live?

ANSWERS: 1. Paul 2. A famous interior designer 3. Deer 4. Smarties 5. Angels 6. The park

---

My Sister Jodie

1. Where do Pearl and Jodie's parents get new jobs?
2. What colour do the girls paint their new bedroom?
3. What do the girls find behind the locked door?
4. What do Pearl and Harley use to attract the badgers?
5. What book does Pearl borrow from Mrs Wilberforce?
6. Tragedy strikes on which night?

ANSWERS: 1. Melchester College 2. Purple 3. Stairs to the tower room 4. Honey 5. The Secret Garden 6. Bonfire Night

---

The Longest Whale Song

1. Who is Ella's best friend?
2. What job does Ella's stepdad do?
3. What does Ella's real dad buy her for a present?
4. What project do Ella, Joseph and Toby work on together?
5. How long did the longest whale song last?
6. Who does Ella fight with at after-school club?

ANSWERS: 1. Sally 2. Teacher 3. Guinea pig 4. The Tudors 5. 22 hours 6. Martha

---

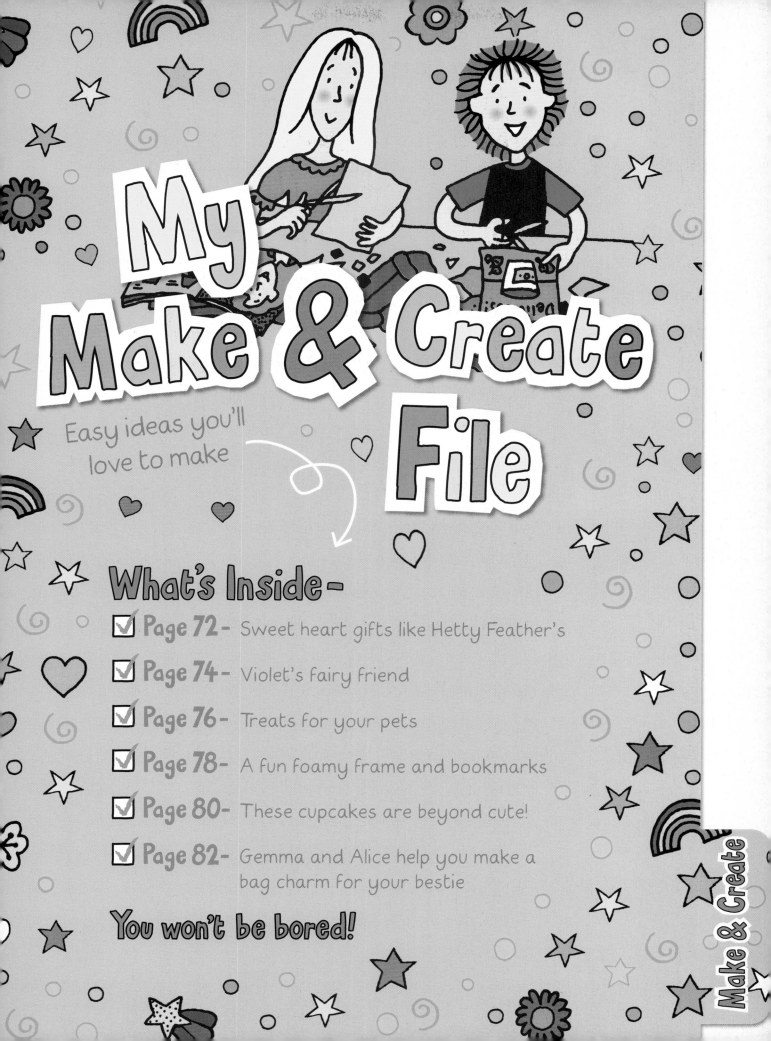

My Make & Create File

Easy ideas you'll love to make

What's Inside-

You won't be bored!

Hetty's Sweet Hearts

Send your love in a heart shape!

You can trace around this heart too!

You'll need:
- Felt
- Buttons and beads
- School glue
- Embroidery thread and needle
- Ribbon

1. Trace these heart shapes and cut patterns from paper. Place the paper patterns on the felt and draw round them. Now cut out the felt hearts.

2. Glue or stitch some buttons and beads on to the felt to make pretty designs. Let the glue dry thoroughly.

Now you can...

Stitch two hearts together with embroidery thread. Stuff the centre with a little cotton wool and some pot pourri before sewing all the way round for scented hearts like Hetty's.

Glue hearts on to cards, note book covers or folders.

Stick two together with a ribbon tie sandwiched between and make them into a bag charm.

Glue them to a plain hair band or stitch on a hair grip.

Stitch a safety pin on the back and transform them into badges.

Button Heart

So easy and so cute!

My Make & Create File

You'll need:

- ❤ Silver coloured jewellery wire reel
- ❤ Pearl buttons pack - natural
- ❤ Pearl buttons pack - blue/green
- ❤ Pearl buttons pack - brown

All available from HobbyCraft

1. Cut a 120cm length of wire and fold in half around a pen or pencil. Twist the wires together and slide the pencil out. Now you have a hanging loop.

2. Thread the buttons one by one on to the double-thickness wire, first up through a single hole, sliding the button into position, then feeding the wire down through the second hole to 'set' the button into position. Start the first button as close to the twist as you can.

3. Continue threading on the buttons, leaving a little finger's width between each, until the last button is within a centimetre or two of the end. Now wrap the end as tightly as possible round the base of the looped wire.

4. Shape the wire into a heart making sure that the hanging loop falls into place in the centre.

Tie some pretty ribbon to the loop for hanging.

Words and pictures courtesy of HobbyCraft.
All products available from

HOBBYCRAFT

For more projects visit www.hobbycraft.co.uk

Violet's Fairy Friend

Make one for your BFF!

Salt Dough

Ingredients:
- 500g plain flour
- 250g salt
- 2 tablespoons cooking oil
- 300ml water

How to make it:

Mix the flour and salt together in a large bowl. Add the oil and water to the mixture. Knead the mixture into a firm dough with your hands. If your dough is sticking to the sides of the bowl, you need to add more flour. If it is too crumbly, add water 2 tablespoons at a time to get the right consistency.

Top Tip!

Build your salt dough model on a sheet of silver foil. You can transfer the sheet to a baking tray once your salt dough figure is finished.

Tools you will need:
- 1 paperclip
- Garlic press
- Butter knife
- Silver foil
- Baking tray
- Rolling pin

1. Turn on your oven to around 80°C (175°F).

2. Roll a golf-ball sized ball of dough for your fairy's body. Flatten it slightly with the palm of your hand and lay it out on a sheet of silver foil.

3. Roll a smaller ball of dough for the head. Fix it to the body with a small dab of water.

4. Mould two small handfuls of dough into two leaf shapes. These will be your fairy's wings.

5. Position the fairy's wings and place the body and head on top. You can dab on a little more water to join the pieces together.

6. Shape two sausage shapes for the arms and attach them to the body. Use a blunt knife to mark in her cuffs. Roll two little balls for your fairy's feet and a tiny ball for her nose. To make the hair, push salt dough through a garlic press or roll long thin strands of dough. Finally, push a paperclip into the top of your fairy's head.

7. Pop your baking tray in the oven for 3–5 hours. Check your dough regularly and take it out when the dough turns golden brown in colour or is baked right through. Leave to cool completely before painting.

8. Time to paint your dough model! Poster paints work best and you can use a fine black pen to add details like the eyelashes. When the paint is completely dry, apply a few layers of clear varnish to protect your finished fairy friend from mould and chips.

Peanut Yum Yums!

Lucky pups will ♥ these easy-peasy dog snacks!

You'll need:

- 210g whole wheat flour
- 190g white flour
- 175g organic or all natural peanut butter
- 240ml water
- 2 tablespoons vegetable oil

1. In a large bowl, mix together the oil, water and peanut butter. Stir in the flour a little at a time.

2. Now use your hands to pull the mix together into a soft dough.

3. Sprinkle some flour on to the work surface and knead the dough until smooth.

4. Roll it out to ½cm thickness and cut out the treats with a small cookie cutter. Place on an ungreased baking tray.

5. Heat the oven to 175 °C and bake the dog cookies for 20 minutes.

Tips!

- Don't give your dog too may treats — one or two a day is enough.
- For an extra-special treat spread a little cream cheese on the biscuits.

*Always ask an adult before using any kitchen equipment

Pet Treat Jar

Paws—itively cute!

Paws off my treats!

You'll need:

- Plain storage jar
- Permanent marker pen
- Coloured modelling clay like Fimo
- Ribbon or coloured string
- Beads

1. Use the permanent marker pen to copy this paw print design on to your jar.

2. Trace and cut out a paper tag pattern from one of the shapes below. Or use a cookie cutter for other shapes.

3. Roll out the clay and cut out rectangle and shape tags like these.

4. Use a wooden skewer to make little holes for ribbon and follow the instructions on the pack to bake (ask an adult to help).

5. When it's cool, write on your pet's name with a marker or metallic pen.

6. Thread the tag and beads on to the ribbon, tie on to the jar then fill with your pet's favourite treats.

Trace these patterns

Tip Add some stick—on sparkles too!

Fun Foam Creations

Hearts & Flowers Frame

Show off your favourite photo in this pretty foam frame.

1. Cut a large heart shape from a sheet of coloured foam. Carefully cut out a smaller heart from the inside to make the basic frame shape.

2. Cut flower shapes from the foam and stick them onto your frame. You can stick gems to the centres of your flowers to add sparkle.

3. Turn your frame over. Cut out a square of foam to make the back of your photo frame. Glue three sides of the square and stick it over the heart shaped opening, leaving the top open so you can slip your photo in at the end.

4. Cut a short length of ribbon and tape it to the back of your photo album to form a loop. You can use this to hang your frame. Now all that's left to do is choose your favourite photo and pop it inside!

Fab Flower Bookmark

Make this amazing bookmark in four easy steps!

My Make & Create File

You'll need:
- A large paper clip
- Card
- Foam
- Sticky foam pads
- Glue
- A sticky gem

1. Draw three different flower templates on a piece of card, then cut them out and trace round them on the coloured foam.

2. Cut out the foam flowers and use the sticky foam pads to fix them together.

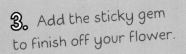
3. Add the sticky gem to finish off your flower.

4. Glue the flower to the paper clip, making sure the slide end of the paper clip is at the bottom.

Tip You could make a bookmark in any shape you like!

79

Cute Critter Cupcakes

So sweet!

Pretty Puppy

You'll need:

- Plain cupcakes to decorate
- Cake cases
- 300g Ready to roll icing
- Icing sugar
- Jam
- Food colouring
- Sweets to decorate

1. Knead a handful of ready to roll icing until it's soft. Sprinkle a clean surface with icing sugar and roll out the icing. Cut a circle to fit the top of your cupcakes.

2. Stick the white icing circle to the top of your cupcake with a thin layer of jam.

3. Add black food colouring to another handful of ready to roll icing and roll it out. Cut out ear shapes and a patch for your puppy's eye and stick them on with a little jam.

4. Use left–over icing to give your puppy eyes and finish with chocolate drops. Add a sweetie nose and laces for the mouth.

Animal-tastic!

You can use these animal design ideas to decorate lots more cupcakes.

Pink Piggy

1. Mix pink food colouring into a large handful of ready to roll icing. Keep a small amount back for the ears. Roll out a circle shape as before and fix this on top of your cupcake with jam.

2. Cut a pink marshmallow in half for the nose. Stick on two chocolate drops for your piggy's nostrils.

3. Cut out ear shapes from the remaining pink icing and stick these at the top of your cupcake. Use a little white icing and more chocolate drops to give your piggy eyes.

Cute Chick

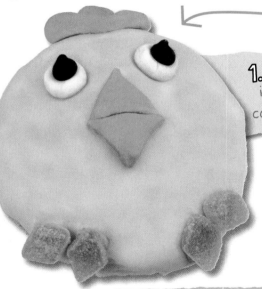

1. Make up yellow icing as before to cover your cupcake.

2. Make up a small handful of orange icing. Cut out two small triangles for the beak and use a little jam to stick them in the middle of your cupcake. Roll three small oval shapes and attach these to the top of your chick's head.

3. Give your chick eyes and push jelly diamonds into the icing for feet.

*Always ask an adult before using any kitchen equipment

BF Secrets Charm

Keep your secrets safe inside!

You'll need:
- Craft foam
- Stick on gems and beads
- Hook and loop fastener dots
- School glue
- Narrow ribbon

1. Cut out the charm template and use it as a pattern to cut the shape from craft foam.

2. Fold as marked and stick a fastener dot on to close. Decorate the charm with foam shapes and stick on gems.

3. Cut out one of the paper strips and fold into a concertina so it fits inside the charm. Glue one end of the strip to the middle section of the charm.

4. Tie on the ribbon as shown, finish the ends with beads and it's ready to tie on to your bag.

Make one for your bestie too!

Now you can have fun adding your BF secrets to both sides of the paper. Here are some ideas –

⭐ Mementoes of places you've visited   ⭐ Photos   ⭐ A poem about best friends

⭐ Secret messages   ⭐ Your signatures

Cut these into three long strips

Cut out this charm pattern

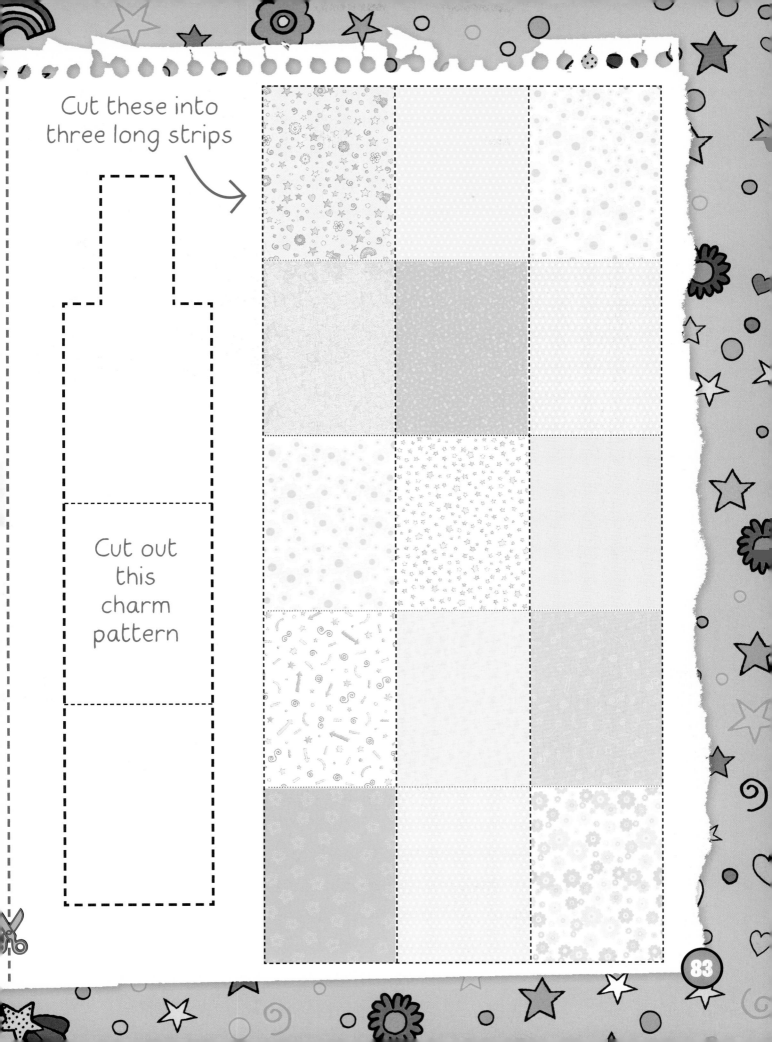

BFF!

A charm to write in your charm!

My name and your name, Folded up together, Tucked up safe inside this charm, To keep us friends forever!

Now sign your names

Jacqueline Wilson

Three's A Crowd

We decided we'd be best friends for ever, Anna-Louise and me. Everyone wanted to be Anna-Louise's friend because she had long yellow hair like a storybook princess and she had big bars of chocolate in her packed lunches and a pink furry pencil case stuffed so full of glittery felt pens it would scarcely stay zipped. She even had a prettier name than anyone else, with its own special hyphen.

She didn't take any notice of me at first. In fact she stuck out her tongue when she saw me staring. But then we were told to be partners for our Ancient Egyptian Artwork project at school. I am often in trouble but I am okay at projects because I have Original Ideas. Everyone else did Pyramids or Mummies but Anna-Louise and I did a Cat Temple. We had cat mummies and weeny kitten mummies and a cat god and lots of cat worshippers, so real looking that everyone wanted to stroke them. I made nearly all the models. Anna-Louise just wrapped bandages, though she did it neatly. My gran still goes on about her missing furry slippers but I hope she won't stay cross forever.

So Anna-Louise and I won a prize and she wound her little finger round mine and we made a pact we would be best friends forever. I got to brush Anna-Louise's hair and share her chocolate bars and draw glittery rainbow pictures.

We went round with linked arms at school and we played every afternoon and we begged to sleep over at each other's houses. So Anna-Louise came to sleep over with me. She had her own turquoise overnight bag with a little turquoise monkey dangling off the end. That gave me the idea for playing jungles with Anna-Louise's luggage monkey and all my old toys. We all wriggled through the great grey jungle under my bed and then cooled off in the steamy pool in the bathroom. My toys are used to my games and can't really get any scruffier, but Anna-Louise's monkey wasn't quite as turquoise when she went home. Her white top and her pale pink shorts weren't quite the same either, though Mum put them in the washing machine.

Anna-Louise and I had great fun giggling half the night but in the morning she got worried about her clothes in case her mum got cross. She wouldn't talk to me when we went down to the corner shop for the newspaper. It's a new family and they don't deliver any more. There's a girl about our age, Amandeep. Sometimes she serves if her mum and dad are busy.

'Who's your friend?' she said.

'Anna-Louise,' I said proudly.

'These aren't my old dungarees,' Anna-Louise said quickly. 'My clothes got all mucked up playing jungles.'

'That sounds a good game,' said Amandeep. She nibbled her lip. 'Can I come and play it too sometime?'

'Sure,' I said, but Anna-Louise shook her head.

'No. It's a game just for us two. Two's company, three's a crowd.'

'Right,' said Amendeep.

It wasn't right. I felt mean. But I was so pleased Anna-Louise and I were still best friends that I didn't want to risk spoiling things by arguing with her.

Anna-Louise's mum pretended not to mind about the clothes but you could tell she was seriously annoyed. I worried that she wouldn't let Anna-Louise stay best friends with me. I tried especially hard to keep in with her. I even let her boss me around a bit. I kept trying to invent new games that she might enjoy. Not mucky games like jungles. I saw this video about girls playing fairies so I made dinky little paper fairies and thank goodness Anna-Louise liked them. Her mother even liked them and strung them up on a mobile in Anna-Louise's bedroom.

'I wish I could see what they look like in your bedroom,' I said.

This was a Big Hint. And it worked. I got invited to sleep over at Anna-Louise's!

'My dad will have to collect his newspaper tomorrow,' I said to Amandeep. 'I'm going to sleep over at my friend Anna-Louise's.'

Amandeep pulled a face.

'I can't stick that Anna-Louise,' she said.

'You're just saying that because you wish you were her friend,' I said.

'Catch me wanting to be her friend,' said Amandeep. 'I don't know what you see in her.'

She stalked into the back of the shop without stopping to serve me.

I decided I didn't care. I was going to sleep over at Anna-Louise's, that was all that mattered. It was going to be wonderful.

It was wonderful at first. She lives in a very big, very clean, very pale house. Anna-Louise's mum likes you to take your shoes off when you get in the front door. And you have to keep rushing off to the bathroom to wash your hands. Still, there's amazing soap and all sorts of special foamy stuff so that's a treat. I played soap bubbles for a bit until Anna-Louise came in and got worried and helped me mop up the puddles. I was surprised because it was a very clean game. Anna-Louise's mum had told me in the car going to her house that we weren't allowed to play any messy games. Especially not jungles.

We had a fantastic tea and then Anna-Louise's mum suggested we make some more fairies. She gave us smooth white paper and a new set of felt tips and lovely sharp scissors. Anna-Louise copied my old fairies. I tried drawing a witch to liven things up but she started to look a little too like Anna-Louise's mum and I knew that wasn't a very sensible idea so I scribbled her over.

I drew Anna-Louise instead. I coloured in her long yellow hair and I dressed her in just a tiny pair of pink and white flowery knickers and then I cut her out very carefully.

'It's me!' said Anna-Louise. 'But why haven't you given me any clothes?'

'Hang on. They're coming next. What would you like?'

I drew her trousers and designer tops and a party dress and a leather jacket and a spangly dance outfit and a ballet frock, all with little tags on the top. Anna-Louise cut some of them out too, but she didn't do it as carefully as me. And then the front door bell went and she cut right through the little paper tags. She didn't seem to care. She ran to the door.

It was this other girl. She had even longer hair than Anna-Louise, all done up in little butterfly clips and bows. She had sparkles on her top and real heels.

'This is Vanessa from up the road,' Anna-Louise said proudly. 'She's come to play too.'

'I don't play,' said Vanessa. 'Do you want me to fix your hair, Anna-Louise?'

'Oh, please!'

'I'll do your hair for you, Anna-Louise,' I said. I whispered in her ear. 'Two's company, three's a crowd!'

But Anna-Louise brushed me away as if I was some bothersome fly.

'What's this?' said Vanessa, snatching up the paper doll. 'Oh, how sweet! You two still play with dollies!'

'No we don't,' said Anna-Louise, going red. 'That was just Laura anyway. She's sleeping over tonight.'

We went up to Anna-Louise's bedroom. Vanessa spent hours doing Anna-Louise's hair. I tried to do my own hair in a fancy way using some old beads but then they got all tangled up and wouldn't come out again and Anna-Louise got cross and said I'd spoilt her special jewellery set.

Then Anna-Louise and Vanessa spent hours going through her wardrobe and mixing and matching outfits. Vanessa said something rude about my dungarees and Anna-Louise giggled. I pretended not to care. Then I unpacked my overnight carrier bag and Vanessa was even ruder about my pyjamas. Anna-Louise couldn't stop giggling.

I stuck my head in the air and pretended I didn't care but I did. When Vanessa went home at long last Anna-Louise was almost nice again and we watched a video on her very own television while my fairies flew round and round our heads on their mobile — but no matter how hard they waved their wands they couldn't make the magic come back.

I stayed awake for hours after Anna-Louise fell asleep.

When I next went to the paper shop Amandeep looked fierce.

'Did you have a good time at your best friend Anna Horrible Hyphen Louise's?' she asked.

'Not really,' I said meekly. 'And as a matter of fact she's not my best friend anymore.'

Guess who my best friend is now! Amandeep and I play together after school and have a seriously wicked time. We make papier-mache models. You need lots and lots of newspaper and paste. Amandeep provides that. You also need Original Ideas. That's my department!

We've made these fantastic savage big bear models. We act out Goldilocks. There's a papier-mache Goldilocks with a pink dress. We have to make lots of papier-mache Goldilocks because the bears bash her on the head and eat her all up.

THE END

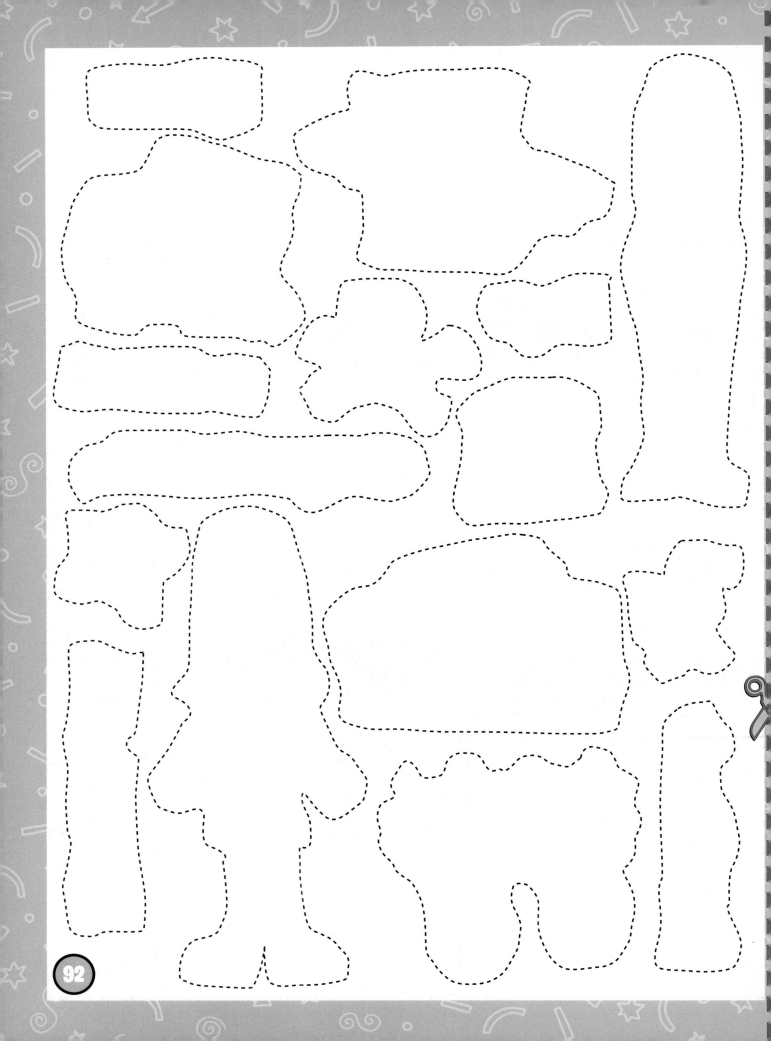

92

Colour 'N' Cut Book Labels

Personalise your favourite books

WARNING!

This book belongs to
....
....

Black belt Tracy

This super book belongs to
....
....

Hi! You're reading ....'s book.

Shh! This totally secret book belongs to
....

This brilliant book belongs to

HANDS OFF! This book belongs to
....